Full Moons
&
Black Cats

Full Moons & Black Cats

Everyday Rules to Guide Your Life

by Terry Boyle

Polar Bear Press, Toronto

Polar
Bear
Press

National Library of Canada Canadian Cataloguing in Publication Data
Boyle, Terry, 1953

    Full Moons & Black Cats: Everyday Rules To Guide
    Your Life
Includes bibliographical references and index.
ISBN 1-896757-20-0

1. Success. 2. Occultism. I. Title. II. Title: Full moons and black cats.

    BF1775.B69 2002   131   C2002-901761-0

Canada

We acknowledge the financial support of the Government of Canada through the Book Publishing Industry Development Program for this project.

Table of Contents

Introduction

My Grandmother, Ethel Annie Cole Boyle, was born in 1889 on a farm in the countryside of Havelock, Ontario. She was a woman who had great faith in, and love for, life. She was also a very wise woman and I had the great joy, when I was a youngster, of sharing her company. Hardly an evening went by without her telling me a story or elaborating on one of her, many, adages.

I accepted every word she said, even though others might have called her beliefs simple superstitions. I thought they were the very foundation of truth and wisdom and they somehow empowered me, despite the ridicule of some of my friends. And she had a saying for everything!

When Grandmother caught sight of a white horse in a field she would hold her left thumb to her lips, then place it on top of her right hand between thumb and index finger, then make a fist with her left hand and pat that spot on her right hand with it. She told me this would bring prosperity to her or to someone close to her so of course I still do this today.

As a young boy I always had a lucky rabbit's foot attached to my belt loop. I truly believed in the power of that amulet; I carried a worry-stone in my pocket to eradicate my problems and I performed all sorts of rituals that would guarantee my safety and good luck. And I wasn't the only one! There was a time when most people felt as I did; adages were common. Good luck was on everyone's agenda.

Every culture has special rituals that were passed from generation to generation like my Grandmother's were passed to me.Did you avoid cracks in the sidewalk, ladders and black cats? Have you forgotten what your own Grandmother taught you? May this book inspire you to recollect and share the expressions and beliefs from your past with your loved ones.

Good luck!

EVERYDAY RULES TO IMPROVE YOUR LUCK

Women should wear yellow underwear on New Year's Eve.

Put salt on the doorstep of a new house
so that no evil can enter.

Make a cross on your right shoulder with the second finger
of your left hand.

Throw coins into a new car for good luck while driving it.

If you find a penny, put it in your shoe and have good luck all day. If you find a penny lying tails up, give it to someone. This will bring you both good luck.

Any house that is inhabited by a frog will be lucky.

Wear new clothes at Easter for good luck all year.

Grow ivy on the outside of your house to protect the inhabitants from witchcraft and evil.

Have your hair cut on Good Friday to prevent headaches for the year.

Hang a horseshoe above the doorway for good luck in your home. In Europe they are placed downward but in most of Britain people believe that the shoes must be turned upward or the luck will run out.

Use the same pencil to take the test as you used to study; the pencil will remember the answers.

Plant rosemary by the doorstep to ward off witches.

Sleep with your head to the north and your feet to the south for deeper sleep.

Hang a horseshoe in the bedroom to keep nightmares away.

Cross your forefingers for good luck.

Carry a rabbit's left hind foot in your left pocket. If it was killed
during a full moon by a cross-eyed person,
your luck will be amazingly good.

A strange black cat on your doorstep will bring you prosperity.

Protect yourself from witches by wearing a blue bead.

Eat breakfast by candlelight on Christmas morning for good luck all year.

If you find the back tooth of a horse, carry it about with you as long as you live and you will never be poor– but you must find the tooth by chance.

Catch a falling leaf on the first day of autumn and you will not catch a cold all winter.

Moles on your back bring money by the sack.

A baby born with a caul, or veil, will be gifted with second sight.

Finding a horseshoe is very good luck indeed but don't give it away—your luck will leave with it.

Carry a handcuff key—it will get you out of trouble.

A baby born with long hair will have a long life.

Knock three times on wood after talking about good fortune
so that evil spirits won't ruin it.

Bury a statue of St. Joseph upside down in your garden and you will sell your house more quickly.

EVERYDAY RULES TO MAKE WISHES COME TRUE

Blow out all the candles on your birthday cake with one puff and your wish will come true.

A wish will come true if you make it while burning onions.

Make a wish when you see the first spring robin but be quick. It will come true only if you finish the wish before it flies away.

Any wish made on a shooting star will come true.

Make a wish while throwing a coin into a well or fountain
and the wish will come true.

When you lose an eyelash put it on the back of your hand, make
a wish and throw it over your shoulder. If it flies off your hand
your wish will come true.

The one who gets the biggest half of a split, dried fowl's 'wishbone' gets their wish.

Meeting a chimney sweep by chance is very lucky. Make a wish when you sight him and it will come true.

Touch blue and your wish will come true.

Never reveal what you have wished—your wish won't come true.

EVERYDAY RULES FOR THE KITCHEN

Salty soup is a sign that the cook is in love.

A fish should always be eaten from the head toward the tail.

When you spill sugar you should dab a bit on your finger
and put it in your mouth to catch the happiness.

While butter is being churned, there must be no bad words, arguing, drinking or singing. Otherwise, the butter will not come to cream.

If you bite your tongue while eating, it is because you have recently told a lie.

A watermelon will grow in your stomach if you swallow a watermelon seed.

A loaf of bread should never be turned upside down
after a slice has been cut from it.

Eat burnt toast for curly hair.

When two people pull apart the dried breastbone of a chicken or
turkey until it breaks, they should each make a wish. The one
with the longest piece will have their wish come true.

Eat an apple a day to keep the doctor away.

Never pass salt across the table from one person to another,
or you will start a fight.

Eating black-eyed peas on New Year's Day brings good luck for
the entire year and if you put a dime in the pot while they are
cooking, it will also bring monetary fortune.

Before slicing a new loaf of bread, make a cross on it.

Eat pork on New Year's Day and you will be fattened with prosperity and money.

If you spill pepper you will have a serious argument with your best friend.

Eating fish will make you smarter.

After eating in someone's home, do not neatly fold your napkin. Leave it crumpled by your plate, otherwise you will never eat there again.

Breaking a plate is an omen of misfortune, especially if it has not already been cracked.

If you eat dessert right before going to bed
you will have nightmares.

It is unlucky to take eggs out of, or bring them into,
a house when it is dark outside.

Do not place shoes upon a table for this will bring bad luck for
the day, cause trouble with your mate and you might even lose
your job as a result.

Don't eat chicken on New Year's Day or you will be scratching for money for the year.

To stir anything with a fork is to stir up misfortune.

It is unlucky to sit on a table unless one foot is touching the ground.

Eat carrots for a good complexion.

Young ladies should not sing while cooking; they are asking for an aged husband.

Eat the skins of Irish or sweet potatoes for rosy cheeks.

Never drink coffee because it will give you a 'muddy' complexion.

Swallow a chicken or turkey heart to acquire beauty.

To enlarge thin legs a woman should wash them every morning with the used dishwater.

Eat egg yolks to improve your colouring.

Lettuce has magical and healing powers including the ability to arouse love and counteract the effects of too much wine. It also aids fertility.

Eat plum pudding at Christmas and avoid losing a friend before next Christmas.

If you refuse mince pie at Christmas dinner you will have
bad luck for the coming year.

When all the food at a meal is consumed,
expect clear weather the next day.

If the cream in milk rises to the top, expect rain.

Lightning and thunder will turn milk sour.

If potatoes burn easily while being cooked, expect dry weather.

If you drop a fork and a spoon and they land across each other, expect a storm.

Crossed knives at table cause quarrels.

After spilling salt throw a pinch over your left shoulder into the face of the devil waiting there.

If 13 people sit down at a table to eat, one of them will die before the year is over.

If a girl eats chicken gizzards she will have large breasts.

Eggs laid on Good Friday never become stale.

EVERYDAY RULES TO WARD OFF DISASTER

Playing with frogs will give you warts.

If you step on a crack, break your mother's back.

Pee in the road, get a sty in your eye.

If you cross your eyes they will stay that way.

Don't bathe while it's storming, you'll be struck by lightning.

Wash blankets in May, you'll wash someone away.

An acorn at the window will keep lightning out.

A swarm of bees on the roof is an omen that the house will burn to the ground.

Never lean a broom against the bed; evil spirits in the broom will cast a spell on it.

Never take a broom along when you move. Throw it out and buy a new one.

To prevent an unwelcome guest from returning, sweep out the room they stayed in immediately after they leave.

Frowning causes wrinkles.

If you play with fire you will wet the bed.

If you count the number of fish you caught you will catch no more that day.

A bed changed on Friday will bring bad dreams.

Don't take a ship that sails on Friday.

Never start to make a garment on Friday unless you can finish it the same day.

Shed no blood on Good Friday, work no wood, hammer no nail.

If a candle lighted as part of a ceremony goes out,
it is a sign that evil spirits are nearby.

Don't drop your comb while combing your hair or
you will soon have a disappointment.

If a friend gives you a knife, give him a coin or your
friendship will be severed.

Don't borrow money on February 1, 2 or 3 as you may be unable to repay it.

Don't lend money on March 29, 30, or 31.

Never put human figures on a quilt; they will walk and visit you at night.

A yawn is a sign that danger is near.

To identify a murderer, get a shoe worn by a young baby who is the same gender as the victim. After the victim has been buried, dig as deeply into the grave as you can near the heart of the victim. Don't touch the coffin or vault. Take a handful of dirt and put it inside the baby's shoe. At midnight burn the shoe and call upon the spirit of the victim to bring the murderer back. Then carry the ashes back to the grave and bury them in another hole in the middle of the grave, above the coffin or vault. In a matter of days, the murderer will be identified.

If a woman walks barefoot during the six weeks following childbirth, her child will have a serious fall when learning to walk.

Get a shoe from the oldest woman you can find. Take it
to your place of business and burn it to a crisp.
This will drive away bad business.

Don't watch an animal defecating or you'll get a
stye in your eye.

Don't put your sweater on inside out.

Don't let your chair fall as you rise from it.

If a candle falls and breaks in two,
double trouble will come to you.

Don't fall asleep with a candle burning.

A candle left to burn itself out will bring misfortune.

It is unlucky and a bad omen to carry fire out of a house
where anyone is ill.

Never give a brooch or pins; it will stab the friendship.

It is bad luck to gaze into a mirror by candlelight,
especially on All Hallow's Eve.

A christening should never be the first event in a new church.

Don't be first to cross a new bridge, it can be a bad omen.

Never put a shoe under the bed and go to sleep;
this will cause nightmares.

Don't kill a ladybug.

Only close a pocketknife if you were the one to open it.

Don't wear a jade ring or necklace.

A baby born with lots of hair will have a troublesome life.

Never stare directly into an animal's eyes. If you look away first it will be very bad luck; if the animal looks away first then you have a bad spirit near you.

Don't sleep with your head toward the door.

Never step over someone; they won't grow.

Don't move into a new house during the months of April, July or November.

To spill ink threatens worry, annoyance and the failure of a project that is underway.

Don't walk under a ladder.

To break a mirror means seven years of bad luck.

Mirrors should be covered during thunderstorms
because they attract lightning.

Get out of bed on the same side that you got in.

When making the bed, don't interrupt your work or you will spend a restless night in it later.

Never start a trip on Friday or you will meet misfortune.

If you weren't born in October, it is unlucky to wear opals.

If a person's garter comes undone it is a warning of treachery.

It is unlucky to give a pair of gloves to a friend unless
you receive something in exchange.

Make sure you give a new pair of shoes to a poor person at
least once during your life or you will go barefoot
in the next world.

It's bad luck to leave shoes upside down. It is unlucky to put on the left shoe before the right and it is worse still to put the right shoe on the left foot, or vice versa.

Never say 'thank you' when someone hands you a knife or you will cut yourself.

It brings bad luck for a flag to touch the ground.

It's bad luck to pick up a coin if it's tails side up.
Good luck comes if it's heads up.

Never say 'thank you' when someone gives you a plant
or the plant will die.

To break a glass bottle means misfortune.

Never give an empty wallet or handbag as a gift;
it will be empty forever.

Never open an umbrella inside a building; it is especially bad
luck if you put it over your head.

It is unlucky to offer your left hand in salutation
as this is a curse to those we hate. We offer our
right hand to those we honour.

Malice and envy are forewarned when sparks jump
out of the fire.

Never disturb the swallows, no matter where they may build
their nests.

Don't bring white lilies into your home.

Lilies of the valley in the garden bring misfortune.

Giving a bunch of lilies of the valley will destroy a friendship.

The full moon can bring on moods of rage or madness.

A red-haired woman is considered unlucky. If a man met a red-haired woman as he was going to work he would certainly forget all about his labours and return home.

Never cross the path of a ploughman.

Posing habitually in front of a mirror will make someone ugly.

Put a red ribbon on a child who has been sick
and the illness won't return.

If you dream of a lizard you have a secret enemy.

If you leave a rocking chair rocking you invite evil spirits
to take your place in the chair.

Don't twist a towel after using it.

If you knock your hand against anything made of iron
it must be taken as a warning against treachery.

Cut your hair on the 17th and 29th of the month to prevent
headaches and baldness.

A baby whose chin quivers will have a bad temper.

Never whistle in the theatre; your next performance will be a total bomb.

Never peek out at the audience before a production.

Never mention by name the play Hamlet in a theatre;
refer to it as the Scottish play.

Never wish an actor good luck; tell an actor to 'break a leg'.

If the palm of your right hand itches it means you will soon be
spending money.

Wearing new shoes on Christmas Day will bring bad luck.

EVERYDAY RULES FOR TRUE LOVE AND MARRIAGE

If your stocking comes down, your lover is thinking of you.

If you accidentally knock your hand against something wooden, you are about to have a love affair.

A girl standing under mistletoe cannot refuse to be kissed by anyone who claims the privilege.

The number of x's in the palm of your right hand is the number of children you will have.

If your lover gives you a knife it means that the love will soon end.

If you drop scissors, it means your lover is being unfaithful to you.

Never put a love letter in your lover's left hand; the love will come to an end.

Knife falls, gentleman calls; fork falls, lady calls; spoon falls, baby calls.

If you secretly put your toenail clippings in a glass of lemonade and make someone drink it, that person will fall in love with you.

To make a lover come to you, stick two pins through the middle of a red candle at midnight and when the candle burns down to the pins the lover will arrive.

Signs you'll fall in love soon:

You stumble up a flight of stairs.
You have hairy legs.
You dream of taking a bath.
The lines on your palm form an 'm'

To dream of what your next boyfriend will look like, try any of the following:

Sleep with a mirror under your pillow.

Wear your nightgown inside out.

Rub your headboard with lemon peel before turning off the light.

Count nine stars each night for nine nights.

Put daisies under your pillow at night.

Sprinkle a sprig of rosemary and a sprig of thyme three times with water and place each herb in a shoe. Put the shoes at the foot of your bed.

Stand in front of a mirror and brush your hair three times before bed.

If your nose itches you will soon be kissed by a fool.

The spouse who goes to sleep first on the wedding day will be the first to die.

To test the fidelity of your lover, light a candle outdoors near his/her house. If the flame burns toward the house or toward you, your lover is faithful.

To see your future husband's face, go to a local spring of water at night carrying a lantern. Peer into the water and see the reflection of his face.

Pansies have magical love powers. The Celts made tea from pansies to use as a love potion. The petals of the pansy are heart-shaped and can cure a broken heart.

Dreaming of a white candle is an omen of true love.

During the day, a young woman must place a broken egg in a glass near a local spring of water in order to see her future husband's face. If she adds some fresh water from the spring and concentrates on the images in the moisture, she will see the face of her prospective husband and those of the children the couple will have.

A red candle in a dream symbolizes passion and sexual desire.

Dreaming of five candles is an omen of love and marriage.

If a single woman sleeps with a piece of wedding cake under her pillow, she will dream of her future husband.

Point your shoes toward the street,
Tie your garters around your feet,
Put your stockings under your bed,
And you'll dream of the man you're going to wed.

If the groom drops the wedding band during the ceremony the marriage is doomed.

On Samhain (October 31) a young woman should light two candles on her dressing table. While in front of the mirror, silently brush her hair and eat an apple. The visage of her future husband will be seen in the glass, looking over her shoulder.

Bridesmaids are dressed in a similar way to the bride for the same reason as the origin of the veil. The bridesmaids are thought to act as decoys to confuse evil spirits and thus protect the bride.

A bride's veil protects her from evil spirits who are jealous
of happy people.

It is the best man's duty to protect the groom from bad luck.
He must ensure that once the groom has begun his journey to
the church he does not return for any reason. He must also
arrange for the groom to carry a small charm in his pocket on
the wedding day. When the best man is paying the church
minister's fee he should pay him an odd sum to bring luck
to the couple.

After the reception the bride throws her bouquet back over her shoulder where her unmarried female guests group together. The one who catches the bouquet will be the next one of those present to marry.

Bride and groom should feed each other wedding cake. This is an omen that throughout the marriage they will feed and care for each other.

When bride and groom toast their new life together they should smash the glasses. That way the glasses will never be used for a better purpose.

When picking a day of the week for a wedding, remember Monday for health, Tuesday for wealth, Wednesday best of all, Thursday for losses, Friday for crosses, Saturday for no luck at all.

If a candle is accidentally knocked out it is a sure sign that there will be a wedding in the near future.

A girl who awakens on her wedding day to the sound of singing birds will never quarrel with her husband.

A spider on the bridal gown or veil is extremely fortunate for it means wealth and plenty.

A bride must not cry before her wedding; this is a bad omen.

A bride should feed a black cat before the ceremony. If the cat rubs itself against her legs this is exceptionally lucky.

To refuse to eat wedding cake means you wish ill of the bride.

Light a white candle on your wedding day to ensure
a long and happy marriage.

On the way to the ceremony it is unlucky to see a funeral procession but very good luck to see a lamb, a toad, a dove or a
spider.

The bride is on the left side of the groom in Christian marriages
so that the groom can have easy access to his sword to defend
his bride from rival suitors.

If a candle should suddenly go out by itself during a wedding ceremony the marriage will surely end in sorrow.

Victorians believed it was lucky to marry on the weekday on which the groom was born. The luckiest day to marry was on the groom's actual birthday.

To ensure happiness the bride and bridegroom should smile at each other when they meet at the altar.

If a bride cries on her wedding day, those shall be the last tears
she ever sheds over her marriage.

Brides should enter the church with the right foot;
to stumble is an omen of evil.

If you are with your beloved and a sparrow flies to your shoulder, a dead relative approves of the relationship. If a sparrow
flies to your head, the relative disapproves.

The bride should not practice walking down the aisle;
she can ask a friend to stand in for her.

Married when the year is new, he'll be loving, kind and true,
when February birds do mate, you wed nor dread your fate. If
you wed when March winds blow, joy and sorrow both you'll
know. Marry in April when you can, joy for maiden and for
man. Marry in the month of May and you'll surely rue the day.
Marry when June roses grow, over land and sea you'll go.
Those who in July do wed, must labour for their daily bread.
Whoever wed in August be, many a change is sure to see. Marry
in September's shrine, your living will be rich and fine. If in
October you do marry, love will come but riches tarry. If you
wed in bleak November, only joys will come, remember. When
December snows fall fast, marry and true love will last.

The new bride must enter her home by the main door and must not trip or fall. It is safest if she is carried across the threshold for the first time.

Tying tins to the back of the newlyweds' car is good luck because the noise will frighten away evil spirits.

If it rains on your wedding day, you'll shed many tears during your married life.

Rain on your wedding day means you will have many children.

Throwing rice wishes the couple fertility and prosperity.

A week before the wedding a house-cat should eat out of the
bride or groom's left shoe.

Tie shoes to the back of the couple's car.

If bridesmaids sign the bottom of the bride's shoe before the wedding, the one whose name is least visible at the end of the day will be the first to marry.

If the groom throws the bride's garter over his shoulder toward the unmarried male guests, the man who catches it will be the next to marry.

If a couple hangs all the decorations from their gifts on the front door for a year they will have good luck.

When the bride is ready to depart for the wedding ceremony a last look in the mirror will bring her luck. Returning to the mirror once she has begun her journey will result in bad luck.

The newly married couple makes the first cut of cake together to symbolize their shared future.

A woman can tell who her future husband will be by standing at the side of the road and watching traffic. She should count ten red cars, then watch for a red-haired girl in a purple dress, then a man in a green tie. The next young man she sees will be her husband.

The bride should wear pearls on her wedding day to ensure she will not cry. In Mexico, it is believed that the bride should not wear pearls on her wedding day for they represent the tears she will cry in her marriage.

If the groom-to-be sees a blind man, a monk or a pregnant woman during his journey to the ceremony he should return home and start the journey again as they are bad luck for him.

It is bad luck to congratulate the bride-to-be; only the future groom should be congratulated.

The bride should not make her own wedding dress. If she does she will cry a tear for every stitch she sews.

The groom should not see the bride in her wedding dress until she arrives at the ceremony.

The bride should never wear her entire outfit before the wedding day. If necessary, she can leave a final stitch on the dress undone until it is time to leave for the ceremony.

If the bride's dress is torn on her wedding day, the marriage will end in death.

For good luck and a lifetime of pleasant relations with the bride's parents, it is advisable for the groom to honour his future mother-in-law with a diamond when he presents the engagement ring to his intended.

The bride-to-be should not remove her engagement ring before the wedding.

If you are married one or two days after a full moon your married life will be filled with good luck.

Engaged women should never let another try on their engagement ring; this is an invitation for the other woman to steal her intended.

Flower girls drop petals as they walk down the aisle to symbolize the many opportunities the couple will have to produce children.

If a young woman sees two white candles in a dream it is a sign that she will soon receive a proposal of marriage.

If sweethearts meet or kiss for the first time under a new moon it is very lucky and they will marry.

When a maiden thinks of her lover and hears a cock crow it signifies their early wedding.

Lovers should meet where there is heather, near a stream or river, on the seashore or in the woods and they will never deceive each other. Poplar trees, however, should be avoided.

Betrothed lovers should not be photographed together or they will be doomed to part or their marriage will be an unhappy one.

On Valentine's Day if a young woman sees a robin flying overhead she will marry a sailor. If she sees a sparrow she will marry a poor man but be very happy. If she sees a goldfinch she will marry a millionaire.

Quarrels and inconstancy are forecast if lovers look together through glass at the new moon.

Lovers should not meet on the stairs and absolutely never kiss or embrace there.

Want to know if you're going to be married in less than a year? Suspend a pea pod (it must have nine peas inside) with white string over the front doorway. If the next person who enters the house by that door is not a member of your family and is single, you will be married in less than a year.

If a young woman loses a garter she will soon have a proposal of marriage.

Want to know how many children you will have? Pick a dandelion that has gone to seed. Blow as many seeds into the wind
as you can. The seeds that remain represent the number of
children you will have.

EVERYDAY RULES FOR GOOD NEWS

If your shoelace keeps coming untied, you will shortly receive a fortunate communication or some kind of good news.

Accidentally putting your stockings or socks on inside out means you will shortly receive a present.

If the bottom of your right foot itches you will soon take a trip.

When a bell rings an angel has just got its wings.

If a bee enters your home you will soon have a visitor. Don't kill the bee or your luck will be bad and the visitor could be unpleasant.

If you sweep trash out the door after dark a stranger will come to visit.

Bees or wasps around the front door indicate wealth.

When your right ear itches it means someone is saying nice things about you. Beware if your left ear itches for the opposite is true.

If your nose itches someone is coming to visit you. Right nostril, female visitor. Left nostril, male.

A quilter should sleep with the finished quilt for one night before giving it to the person for whom it was made.

If you dream of a candle in a holder it symbolizes a happy and prosperous future.

A baby who looks like his mother will have good luck.

A baby born with an open hand will have a generous disposition.

The child born on Christmas Day will have a special fortune.

If you catch your clothes on bushes or a briar while out walking you will have a monetary gain.

A horse with white 'stockings' is very lucky and even more so if it has a white 'star' on its forehead.

Good luck will come to the home where a fire is kept burning throughout the Christmas season.

A blowing wind on Christmas Day brings good luck.

EVERYDAY RULES FOR GOOD HEALTH

Mistletoe in the house protects it from thunder and lightning and can cure many diseases, is an antidote to poison and brings good luck and fertility.

If a fly falls on your food immerse it once more; the fly carries the antidote on one wing for the poison on the other.

Wear an amber necklace to protect against illness or cure colds.

Cut an onion in half and place it under the bed of a sick person and it will draw off fever and poison.

Make a visit to your birthplace late in life and your life will be prolonged.

Sleep with a quilt if you are unwell and the love from that quilt will help to heal you.

If you suffer from nosebleeds, tie a pure lead ball on a ribbon and wear it around your neck so that it falls in the gully of your throat. Your nosebleeds will stop.

Place a knife under the bed during childbirth and it will cut the pain of labour.

To cure ague tie a few spiders in a bag and wear it around your neck. This will cure fever but no one except a fairy doctor should untie or open the bag or the charm will be broken.

Put a ring on a string and hold it over a pregnant woman's abdomen and you can tell the sex of the unborn child. If the ring swings to and fro it's a boy; if it swings in a circle, it's a girl.

Put olive oil and pepper on a piece of cotton ball and insert it in your ear to get rid of an earache.

Lemon and whiskey take away a cough.

To cure a fever, place the patient on a sandy shore when the tide is coming in and retreating waves will carry away the disease.

To cure tonsillitis, apply a stocking filled with hot potatoes to the throat.

If you have rheumatism you should carry a wizened potato in your hip pocket to relieve the pain.

Children born when there is a full moon must be careful with
their health.

Keep cats away from babies because they will suck the breath of
the child.

To have good health throughout the next year, eat an apple on
Christmas Eve.

Lettuce promotes fertility if eaten by young women and certain types of salad can bring on labour in pregnant women.

Mandrake root has aphrodisiac and fertilizing properties, prevents sterility and barrenness and compels love.

If you eat a raw egg before eating anything else on Christmas morning you will be able to carry heavy weights.

EVERYDAY RULES FOR BEAUTY

Rise before the sun on the first three mornings of May and
cover your face with dew.

Bathe your face in March snow water.

Squeeze the tip of a finger to see the colour of cheek rouge
you should wear.

Wipe your face every morning with a baby's wet diaper.

Each morning lie on the bed and rest your ankles on the foot-board; this will ensure slim ankles.

Eat chicken or turkey hearts.

Wash your hands with your own urine.

To get rid of freckles, put the blood of a bull or hare on your face. The distilled water of walnuts is also good for this purpose.

Wash your face each morning with your first urine.

If a girl's petticoat or slip shows below her dress, she is loved more by her father than her mother.

EVERYDAY RULES TO OBSERVE WHEN THERE IS A DEATH

Light twelve candles around a corpse to protect the soul of the deceased from evil forces; ghosts and demons cannot cross into a circle of lighted candles.

Nothing new should be worn to a funeral, especially new shoes.

Hold your breath while going past a cemetery or you will breathe the spirit of someone who has recently died.

If a woman is buried in black she will return to haunt the family.

Lift your feet when you ride past a cemetery because the people buried there will sneak their spirits into your body.

Never count the cars in a funeral cortege.

Don't meet a funeral procession head on.

If the person buried lived a good life, flowers will grow on the grave. If the person was evil, weeds will grow.

The soul of a dying person can't escape the body and go to heaven if any locks are locked in the house.

Thunder following a funeral means that the dead person's soul has reached heaven.

All windows should be opened at the moment of death so that the soul can leave.

Pregnant women should not attend funerals.

To encounter a grave-digger coming toward you is a very evil portent, usually forewarning a serious illness.

Whippoorwills call for the souls of the dead.

If you touch a loved one who has died you won't have dreams about them.

A drip of wax down the side of a candle at a séance means bad luck or death to the person nearest that side of the candle.

If a cat appears on a grave that person's soul is in the Devil's power.

It is very unlucky to enter a house through the back door and leave by the front; that is the route used by funerals.

When somebody dies the clocks in the house should be stopped, the curtains drawn and the mirrors covered over. If a mirror is left uncovered the next person who sees their image will be the next to die.

Anyone who dies on Good Friday or at midnight on Christmas Eve will go straight to heaven because the gates of heaven are open then.

If the deceased's eyes are left open he'll find someone to take with him.

All windows should be opened at the moment of death so that the soul can leave.

When you hear of one death you will soon hear of two more.

It's unlucky to kill a sparrow because they carry the souls of the dead.

Light a candle on the night after November 1 for each deceased relative and place it in the window of the room where the death occurred.

EVERYDAY RULES THAT FOREWARN DEATH

Dropping an umbrella on the floor means there will be a murder in the house.

When a bat enters the house after dark someone in that house will not be there on the following night.

Never put your hat on the bed; you will be seriously injured or even killed.

Don't sleep on feather pillows because after a time a ball of feathers will form under your head and when the feathers form a complete circle, you will die.

If a white dove flies at the windshield of your car someone in your household will die a natural death soon.

If you say goodbye to a friend on a bridge you will never see each other again.

Two deaths in the family mean that a third is sure to follow.

When someone is leaving always turn away before they are out of sight or you will never see them again.

If three people are photographed together, the one in the middle will die first.

There will be a death soon if:

A curlew cries or an owl hoots.

There is a knock on the wall near the bed of an invalid.

You take photographs of someone in their casket.

You point at a funeral procession you will die within the month.

A candle suddenly goes out by itself.

A candle flame burns blue.

You dream of a black candle.

There is a bird in the house.

You see an owl in the daytime.

You dream about a birth.

A sparrow lands on a piano.

Scissors fall and come to rest point down.

A dog howls outside your house.

A black beetle runs over your shoe.

You see a cockroach in an unusual place.

A robin flies into a room through a window.

A raven flies on your left and calls.

There is a single magpie to your left.

Magpies fly past your house.

A clock which has not been working suddenly chimes.

Your left eye twitches.

A mirror falls and breaks by itself.

A white moth is inside the house or tries to enter the house.

Three seagulls fly together, directly overhead.

The first person seen by a cat that has wiped its face with its paws will be the first in the household to die,

A black cat crossing your path by moonlight means death in an epidemic.

If a bird pecks on your window or crashes into it there has been a death.

Funerals on Friday mean another death in the family during the year.

EVERYDAY RULES FOR THE WEATHER

Red sky at night, soldiers' delight; red sky at morning, soldiers are mourning.

Regardless of the weather on Saturday, there will always be enough sunshine to dry a workingman's shirt.

March winds and May sun make linen white and ladies dumb.

If the sun rises red in summer expect a very hot day.

When a dog or horse rolls on the ground there will be a change in the weather.

To see a large flock of crows means a change of weather.

Lightning in the south indicates dry weather.

When horses race around and play there will be a change
in weather.

The wood of a tree that was struck by lightning is very unlucky.

When the sun rises in the southeast look for a cool summer.

The direction taken by a shooting star indicates the direction of the wind the following day.

When you hear a number of owls hoot at the same time during the day there will be a change in the weather.

Whirlwinds of dust in the spring indicate a dry summer.

When pigeons are more restless than usual and continually coo, there will be a change in weather.

Whatever the weather is on Friday at noon the weather for the following Sunday will be the same.

EVERYDAY RULES TO FORECAST RAIN

Rain is coming if:

A crescent moon has its points tilting downward and cannot hold water.

Your broken bone aches.

The moon hides behind a thin veil of mist.

Your nose itches three times within an hour.

Cows lift their tails.

You drop a piece of buttered bread and it falls buttered-side down on the floor.

You step on a spider indoors.

Your clothes will not take starch.

The leaves on trees curl up.

Snakes begin to leave the water.

The wind is in the east.

You kill a snake and lay it on its back.

Dandelion blossoms close.

Sea gulls fly inland.

There are a great many women on the street.

The tobacco in a man's pipe becomes hot and sticky and the pipe does not draw well.

Frogs croak during the day.

A cat washes its face around the ears.

A snake crosses your path.

The sound of horses' hooves can be heard more clearly than usual.

When tree frogs call from a tree it will rain within three days.

When the moon lies on its back the following month will be wet.

Swarming gnats mean warmer weather and rain.

Thunder before noon means rain in the afternoon.

Two stars within the ring around the moon mean rain within two days.

Use the telephone during a rainstorm and you will get a shock.

If corns hurt a thunderstorm is near.

If a flock of wild geese fly westward and do not turn southward or northward when it reaches a town there will be a great flood in that town within a day or two.

If the clouds open before seven and close afterward, it will rain by eleven.

If it rains on Easter it will rain for seven days.

When there is lightning in the north it will rain within 24 hours.

Put lime under the eaves of your house and you will have rain that day.

When a rooster sits on a fence and crows very early in the morning it will rain before breakfast.

Wind in the east during early winter or late spring means either snow or rain.

When sunshine and rain come together it will rain at the same time on the following day.

The north wind on New Year's Day is the sign of a wet summer.

EVERYDAY RULES FOR STORMY WEATHER

When a storm is coming, lie on your back by a tree and the lightning will not hit you.

When chickens roost low a storm will come the next day.

There will be a storm before Wednesday when the sun is obscured by clouds at sundown on Sunday.

If a rooster crows at midnight there will be bad weather.

When you see a big storm in the sky, quickly put the point of an axe in the ground and it will cut the storm in two.

Red sky at night, sailor's delight; red sky in the morning, sailors take warning.

Don't keep a piece of iron or steel like a pocketknife or a hatpin on your person for it will draw lightning during a storm.

Thunder in the morning is a sailor's warning.

If cattle in winter come running from the pasture, there is going to be a blizzard within 24 hours.

Lightning never strikes twice in the same place.

Make children sit on feather pillows during a storm so that lightning will not strike them.

Never leave windows up during a storm; a draft blowing through the house will draw in lightning.

If you kill a bullfrog you can expect foul weather the next day.

Burn blessed candles during a storm for protection.

It's safe to sit in an automobile during a storm because the rubber tires will protect against lightning.

A mule rolling at midday is the sign of a storm before midnight.

Lightning will never strike a person who is sleeping nor will it hit a house in which a fire is burning.

You can expect foul weather if a rooster crows while sitting on the ground.

Wild ducks flying low indicate falling weather.

There will be a storm when:

Fish jump wildly.
A cow raises her tail over her back and runs.
There is a ring around the moon.
A teakettle boils dry.
Cattle crowd together.

EVERYDAY RULES FOR SNOW AND WINTER

You may look for snow next day if the sun appears during a snowfall.

When robins arrive, spring is here.

Whatever direction the wind is blowing on New Year's Day will be its direction for the next three months.

When a snipe starts to cry winter has been broken.

Winter will come late if wild ducks do not go south
until late autumn.

Yellow butterflies in the autumn indicate a frost within ten days
that will tint the leaves the same colour.

When the wind is in the east it is not the time for man
nor beast.

The itching of frostbitten feet is the sign of snow.

Whenever there is a fog in January, expect a frost on the same
day in May.

The weather during the first twelve days of the year indicates what the weather will be all year.

The direction of the wind on the first three days of December indicates how it will blow during the three following months.

Thunder in February is the sign of snow in May.

The weather of the first three days of any season denotes the weather for the season.

To determine the number of big snowfalls for the year, count how many days old the moon is at the first appearance of snow.

If a fire crackles gently like the falling of hard granular snow, you will soon see a snowstorm of this kind.

If snowflakes are small it will continue to snow.

If snow has stuck to the sides of trees, it will snow again within a few hours.

It will snow within 24 hours if there are two circles around a full moon.

Large, bright stars in winter mean frost next morning.

Large snowflakes mean that the snow will not last long.

If hogs begin to build their beds or pigs pull hay from a haystack to make a nest, look for cold weather.

During winter, if rabbits are in brush piles, the weather will become colder.

Snowbirds flying along a rail fence indicate that the weather will turn colder within 24 hours.

A white Christmas foretells a green Easter.

Six weeks of cold weather may be expected if sparrows mate in March.

When caterpillars during the autumn are dark brown in the center of their bodies and are yellow at each end, the middle of the winter will be very cold.

There will be eight more weeks of cold weather if a ground hog can see his shadow on the 2nd of February.

If sheep turn their backs to the wind, there will be a cold spell.

Insects carrying material for nests indicate that cold weather is approaching.

A cold winter foretells a hot summer.

It will be a cold, hard winter if:

There is a circle around the moon.
A muskrat's nest is built deep in the ground.
Wild fruits are plentiful in the autumn.
The fur of animals in the autumn is thick and heavy.
Wild geese fly high on their way south.
The goose has a long breastbone.
Animals build their beds early in the autumn.
The hulls on walnuts are tight.
When hogs are slaughtered early in the fall and their lungs are streaked.
Flowers, which normally blossom but once a year, bloom twice during the season.
The breastbone of a goose is dark.
Squirrels bury their nuts deep in the ground.
Raccoons are fat during the autumn or early winter.

Muskrats cut corn stalks and carry them underground.
There is a heavy crop of wild grapes.
There is a large crop of hazelnuts.

Thunder while trees are bare foretells cold weather.

Thunder in the winter is a sign of colder weather.

Thunder on the 14th of January means frost on the 14th of May.

Thunder on the 6th of February signifies a frost on the 6th of May.

Thunder in the latter part of February or early March means that a cold spell is near.

Two sun dogs mean bad weather.

Unusually warm weather during the first week of August
indicates a white winter.

We are going to have cold weather if the wind sweeps down
the chimney.

If a fire sighs very cold weather is coming.

If a gate incessantly opens and slams cold weather is near.

In winter if turkeys are at the top of the roost it will be cold, in the middle of the roost not very cold and if they remain on the ground it will not be cold at all.

EVERYDAY RULES FOR GOOD NEWS ABOUT WEATHER

Expect fair weather if a fog does not lift but evaporates.

Winter will arrive late when wild ducks do not go south until late autumn.

When the wind is in the west it will never rain.

When spotted clouds that look like a flock of sheep gather in the west this is an indication that the weather will clear soon.

Ring around the sun, rain none.

When birds and insects mate in August we will have a late fall.

If the sun sets clear we will have beautiful weather
for three days.

The weather will be warmer if we have a sun dog in the evening.

Weather will be clear if the wind is in the south
and the sky is cloudy.

Thunder after leaves have appeared on the trees
means warm weather.

A new moon on Monday means the weather will be good.

If there is a rainbow in the east we shall have dry weather.

Fair weather may be expected for the following day if the setting sun reflects from windows.

A clear and sharp train whistle means fair weather.

A clear, star-filled sky on Christmas Eve will bring good crops in the summer.

The winter will be mild if:

Onions in the autumn have thin skins.

Beavers build a small lodge for the winter.

The nut crop fails.

Hogs are slaughtered in early autumn and the small part of the
spleen lies toward the head.

Caterpillars in the fall are light-coloured.

Worms stay near the surface of the ground in winter.

Walnut hulls are loose and easily removed.

Corn silk is thin and scanty.

Caterpillars are completely black in the autumn.

You can easily remove the inside of a chicken gizzard.

The goose has a white breastbone.

Terry Boyle has been a journalist, broadcaster and teacher for over 30 years. He also conducts popular 'Historical Ghost Tours', re-tracing the history and hauntings of Parry Sound.
More information can be found at www.sundogtours.ca.

Your comments and any beliefs or sayings you wish to pass on would be appreciated. You may contact Mr. Boyle at:
www.north49@idirect.com
or
c/o Polar Bear Press
35 Prince Andrew Place
Toronto, Ontario
M3C 2H2